IT'S **ALWAY**  DAY TO BE THE **BOSS**

THE BOSS

SOURCEBOOKS HYSTERIA™
AN IMPRINT OF SOURCEBOOKS, INC.®
NAPERVILLE, ILLINOIS

CHARLOS GARY

Published by Sourcebooks Hysteria, an imprint of Sourcebooks, Inc.

P.O. Box 4410, Naperville, Illinois   60567-4410

(630) 961-3900

FAX: (630) 961-2168

www.sourcebooks.com

ISBN: 1-4022-0800-6

ISBN 13: 978-1-4022-0800-3

Printed and bound in the United States of America

CH 10 9 8 7 6 5 4 3 2 1

INTRODUCTION

I used to think there was nowhere in America worse than the inner-city neighborhood where I spent my childhood. When I was young, I often fantasized about working in one of those big skyscrapers downtown and going to work every day in a suit and tie. Back then, my image of the white-collar world was based on what I had seen on television: nice suits, coffee breaks, business cards, expense accounts, cheerful meetings, and savvy business types.

Then, I entered the world of corporate America. I soon realized that corporate life was quite different from what I had imagined. The relationships between managers and employees were often strained, and it was difficult to figure out whom I could and could not trust.

One day, when I was feeling particularly frustrated by my job, a colleague suggested that I create a cartoon about the world of office life. *Working It Out* was born!

Finally, I had an outlet for some of my frustrations. It was like good therapy, only with a pen and paper instead of an actual therapist. Suddenly, I couldn't wait to go to work the next morning! My source of anxiety became my daily inspiration, and people at work started to take notice. I started doing strange things—like paying attention during long meetings that had once seemed pointless and boring. The corporate world had become my fodder, and I was taking copious notes.

If you're stuck in a small cubicle and feeling discouraged about your job, you're not alone. I hope these cartoons will give you a little joy as you try to make it through another day at work.

Here's to corporate America!

"I hope you don't mind, but we've decided to have our meeting in your cubicle."

"Well, I'm off to the executive planning meeting."

"Hello, Mr. Jamison? The Valentine's
Day chocolates that you mailed
to yourself have just arrived."

"Your salary expectations are much too high. I was thinking of a figure in the range of nothing."

"Sure, you can get this project finished
on time. Just call your wife and tell her
that you won't be home for a few weeks."

"I need to practice my golf swing.
Can you place your head on the X?"

"The focus group says we need to appeal to a younger demographic."

"My mood swings vary depending on
how well my stocks are performing."

"Don't worry, Smith. This project is a no-brainer."

"Sure, I've learned something from today's session. I've learned that you're grossly overpaid."

"When you're finished with those documents, do you mind filing my nails?"

"Since your boss lives alone, I decided to invite him over for dinner. Is that OK, honey?"

"Considering that I employ your parents,
I think that I deserve some kind of a treat."

"The top line represents the economy, the bottom line is our profits, and that line across the street is unemployment."

"Hello, boss? I'm calling in sick
today. I think I caught something."

"Seriously, boss. It makes
you look ten years younger."

"Okay, I'm ready to listen to your ideas."

"They're not really ID cards.
They're employee tracking devices."

"You've been disappointing in your last
few tasks. It's time you raised the bar!"

"C'mon, Jack. You're not going to let something trivial like ethics stand in the way of a successful management career?"

"The boss said that he'd consider giving
me a promotion if I agreed to play horsey."

28

"I'm in my eighth month of pregnancy.
How far along are you?"

"I have a very important assignment for you today. It's called 'picking up my dry cleaning.'"

"I'm glad you finally see things my way.
You know, it takes a big man to admit
when he's wrong."

"I had to cancel my trip to Brazil because
they require a visa for entry. I only have an
American Express card."

"I have to make confetti for my nephew's birthday party. Can you please shred this stack of resumes?"

"I don't want to point fingers, but
somebody in this room just cost the
company a million-dollar account!"

"One of my employees has accused
me of being closed-minded. He's just
upset because I refuse to listen to him."

"Rogers, I need you to write a
5,000-page report on wasting time!"

"Seriously, Jamison. Your new combover
looks a thousand times better than mine."

"Congratulations, Wilson! You've won this
year's brown-noser-of-the-year award!"

"Sir, I've discovered why your new laptop
isn't working properly. It's called user error."

"My broker told me to invest in small caps."

"Boss, I'd like you to meet my mother,
Julia. Mom, this is my boss, Satan."

"You're all set for your Cleveland trip.
To save money, I've made arrangements
for you to sleep on a local park bench."

"He's not sleeping at his desk, sir. He's trying
to clean the keyboard with his tongue."

"Margaret, I just realized that I don't have any friends. Could you hire some for me?"

"You're a nice guy, but I'm looking for someone more financially secure. Is your boss single?"

"Are you sure that giving you a sponge
bath is part of my internship duties?"

"I'm sorry, Mr. Jamison. You can't claim
your employees as dependants."

"Geez, boss! Just when I was starting to enjoy
this job, you come along and wake me up!"

"Margaret, I have to make a PowerPoint presentation in five minutes. Can you teach me how to use PowerPoint?"

"Actually, I'm only half-peon, sir. My
mother is 100 percent management."

"Shouldn't somebody tell the intern
that he's sitting in the boss' chair?"

"The boss says that he's going to take away my Internet access. I guess I'll just have to find other ways to goof off."

"It's nice to meet you, Mr. Nelson. I can see
where your son gets his stupidity from."

"Maybe someone should tell the boss
to turn down the air conditioner."

"Remind me to start losing weight
after the holidays. Two kids tried to sit
on my lap at the mall yesterday!"

"My employee, Jorge, calls me 'el estupido.'
He says that's Spanish for 'excellent boss.'"

"Margaret, I'm taking a long lunch break.
Tell the staff that I'll be back in a few days."

"Listen up, fellas. The winner gets to take
the lead on that important project."

"Wow! The reception on this island is really great, boss. It's like you're here on vacation with me."

"I built a graveyard next to this building just
in case I accidentally work someone to death."

"No matter how hard I try, I just
can't get the boss off my back."

"Say, Carter, did you get a chance
to fax that important memo?"

"Your organizational skills are excellent,
but I'm a little concerned about your
declining butt-kissing skills."

"Nelson, I'm giving you this very important project. You have 10 minutes to complete it."

"My niece will be working here as an intern, so I'm giving her your cubicle. Do you mind working in the bathroom for a few months?"

"Sorry, kid. Interns aren't allowed
to sit at the big conference table"

"Human resources told me to remind you idiots about next week's sensitivity training seminar!"

"Harrison told me that you stole his proposal
idea. If that's true, I have no choice but
to promote you to management!"

"Looks like our CEO lost his wallet again."

"Sorry, I can't remember your name.
Do you mind if I just call you 'stupid'?"

"I need you to re-write this report again.
The last 50 you submitted were unacceptable."

"Mr. Jamison, I really didn't mean any of those terrible things that I said about you in the company newsletter."

"No, I don't have anything
better to do. Why do you ask?"

"Why don't you just retire, already?!"

"People, we must put an end to bathroom breaks. That wasted time cost the company almost $50,000 last year!"

"The EPA says that our production facility is an environmental hazard. On a brighter note, we've finally made the cover of *Pollution Digest*."

"I guess you can call it a celebration.
The boss called in sick today."

"I'll give you $10,000 if you agree to throw out the bribery charge."

"We're not hiring right now, but you're more than welcome to come in and work for free."

"This is my last day working here,
so I'm going to need a good reference.
How much do you charge?"

"I would have told you about the deadline, but I didn't want to bother you with useful information."

"You've worked really hard this year, but
I've decided to give the new management
position to my 6-year-old niece."

"I'm bringing in a new job candidate today.
I want you all to pretend that you're happy here."

"Good luck in your big meeting, sir."

"My therapist said that I needed to
work off some pent-up aggression."

"You can check my references, but if I were you,
I wouldn't believe anything that those liars say."

"I could tell you that it was nice to meet you,
but then I'd just be lying."

"Little Jimmy here says that he wants to be a loser when he grows up. So, naturally, I wanted him to meet you."

"Okay, the 4-week honeymoon is over! It's time I started treating you like a regular employee!"

"As you can see, 25% of our customers dislike
our product, while 75% of them hate it."

"Judging by your smile, I'm guessing that you picked me to work the weekend shift."

"Sorry, but you're not getting business cards.
I only give them to important people."

"Hello, employment agency? Can you send over a new temp? I think I broke the last one."

"So, when you said 'black tie only,'
you meant the whole suit?"

"Sorry, you're just not a good fit here."

"Sorry, but you can't include your
pets on your personal reference list."

"What's wrong, Mitchell?
You don't like your new office?"

"When I count to 3, you'll become a productive,
competent, and efficient worker."

"To continue with our 'Mindless Meetings'
series, we're going to discuss proper
pencil-sharpening techniques."

"Greetings, little one. Meet your new corporate sponsor."

"Don't worry, Jackson. It's just
part of the interview process."

"I couldn't think of anything to buy
you, so I got you this lovely pink slip."

"I wanted to feel important,
so I bought a bigger chair."

"You'll never go far in this company unless
you stop letting people walk all over you!"

"You know, you and I have something in common. We're both very powerful men."

"I had a really tough workout this morning.
I spent a full minute on the treadmill."

"Sure, kid, I like the product. But you need to work on your sales pitch."

"Welcome aboard, Ms. Hudson. Please accept this roll of quarters as your signing bonus."

"Trust me, Mr. Jamison. Humans
can't catch a computer virus."

"YOUR accomplishments, YOUR achievements, blah, blah, blah ... Look, son, if you really want this job you'd better start talking about me!"

"I think that now would be a good
time to discuss my promotion, sir."

"I promised you a raise at the office party?
Surely, you can't hold me responsible for
the things I say when I'm drunk."

"You really dropped the ball
on your last assignment."

"It's part of Mr. Jamison's plan
to eliminate fun in the workplace."

"This baseball bat has sentimental value to me. I used it to bust up a few labor unions."

"My boss put this electric shock collar around my neck to keep me from wandering outside of my sales territory."

"Actually, sir, you DO pay me
to talk on the phone all day."

"OK, everybody repeat after me ... "

"So, we're in agreement that your main
goal for the next year is to do some work."

"Since you'll only be working part time here,
I've decided to give you half of a workstation."

"Sir, your branch manager is here to see you."

"For his consistent pursuit of bonehead ideas, the Manager of the Year award goes to Mr. Jamison."

"My secretary is off sick today."

"Let's take a break from this meeting to allow Mr. Rivers to finish his doodling!"

"Look, I don't want you to waste your
time coming up with a good idea, because
you'll eventually end up doing it my way."

"Finally! Someone in this office is
showing me the respect I deserve!"

"I tried to give him money, but he insists on being paid in bubble-wrap."

"Margaret, tell the custodian that we've run out
of paper towels in the executive washroom."

"Well, now you've done it, Jamison! You told him to think, and it caused his head to explode!"

Charlos Gary is a nationally syndicated cartoonist with Creators Syndicate. His first published cartoon was a comic strip entitled *State U.*, which ran in the Ohio State University student newspaper. His first professional cartoon appeared in the Elmira, New York, *Star-Gazette*, thus launching his career as a cartoonist. In 1999, he earned a Pulitzer Prize nomination for his graphic artwork at the Arlington Heights, Illinois, *Daily Herald*. Today, his cartoon series, *Working It Out*, appears weekly in over thirty-five newspapers nationwide. Charlos lives in St. Petersburg, Florida, with his wife, Agustina.